FOUNDATI

The US Co
and Bill of

by Maegan Schmidt

Content Consultant
Robert Allison, Professor of History
Suffolk University

CORE
LIBRARY

Published by ABDO Publishing Company, PO Box 398166, Minneapolis, MN 55439. Copyright © 2013 by Abdo Consulting Group, Inc. International copyrights reserved in all countries. No part of this book may be reproduced in any form without written permission from the publisher. The Core Library™ is a trademark and logo of ABDO Publishing Company.

Printed in the United States of America,
North Mankato, Minnesota
112012
012013

 THIS BOOK CONTAINS AT LEAST 10% RECYCLED MATERIALS.

Editor: Blythe Hurley
Series Designer: Becky Daum

Cataloging-in-Publication Data
Schmidt, Maegan.
 The US Constitution and Bill of Rights / Maegan Schmidt.
   p. cm. -- (Foundations of our nation)
Includes bibliographical references and index.
ISBN 978-1-61783-763-0
1. United States. Constitution--Juvenile literature. 2. United States--Politics and government--1775-1783--Juvenile literature. 3. United States--Politics and government--1783-1789--Juvenile literature. I. Title.
342.7302--dc22

                                        2012946539

Cover: This painting, created in 1878, shows the delegates signing the Constitution of the United States.

CONTENTS

CHAPTER ONE

The Road to Revolution

The American colonies were started during the 1600s. The people who lived there had crossed the Atlantic Ocean to begin a new life. Over time, these colonists created their own laws and way of life. But they were still ruled by the British Empire.

Many of the colonists began to dislike following the rules of a country so far away. The British

British troops fire at colonists in Lexington, Massachusetts. This battle in 1775 was the first battle of the Revolutionary War.

government made laws to tax the colonists. But the colonists did not have representatives voting for them in Parliament. Parliament was Great Britain's law-making body. Many colonists believed this was wrong. They wanted their own local governments to make their laws.

The Declaration of Rights and Grievances

Angry colonists sent King George III a document called the *Declaration of Rights and Grievances* in 1765. The colonists told King George they still owed him loyalty and obedience. But they also believed they had certain rights the king should protect. The people wanted representation in their own country. They wanted to pay taxes created by their own governments.

The First Continental Congress

In 1774 representatives came to a meeting called the First Continental Congress in Philadelphia, Pennsylvania. This group sent a message to King George III and the British government. It asked them to end their unfair laws. King George III

King George III—ruler of Great Britain leading up to and during the Revolutionary War—in his royal attire

said no. He wanted the colonies to obey Great Britain, even if it meant a war.

The Revolutionary War Begins

By 1775 more colonists wanted to be free of British rule. These people called themselves patriots. They believed the colonies should become an independent nation. Many colonists prepared for war. On April 19, 1775, British soldiers and colonists fought in Lexington, Massachusetts. This was the start of the Revolutionary War.

Representatives at the Continental Congress sign the Declaration of Independence.

The Second Continental Congress

Representatives met for the Second Continental Congress in May 1775. Some still hoped to stop the war. They wrote a letter called the Olive Branch Petition to King George III. They asked him to stop the fighting until the two sides could reach an agreement. The king said no. The colonists knew they would have to fight.

Declaring Independence

In 1776 Congress named Benjamin Franklin, John Adams, Roger Sherman, Robert Livingston, and Thomas Jefferson to write a declaration of independence. Jefferson was the document's main author. The document explained why the colonies should become an independent nation. Congress approved the declaration on July 2, 1776. But the colonists would still have to win the Revolutionary War to earn their freedom.

EXPLORE ONLINE

This chapter had a lot of information about the colonists' growing anger toward British control. You can find even more information about this anger over the Stamp Act of 1765 at the Web site below. Compare and contrast the information on the Web site with the information in this book. Why were the colonists angry with these laws? What actions did they take?

Boston Mob Protests Stamp Act
www.massmoments.org/moment.cfm?mid=236

CHAPTER TWO

The Articles of Confederation

The Declaration of Independence said the United States of America was independent of Great Britain. But it did not create a central government. Each colony became a state with its own government.

When Congress members wrote the Declaration of Independence, they also created a document called the Articles of Confederation. It was not adopted by

Original copies of the Declaration of Independence, the Articles of Confederation, the Bill of Rights, and the Constitution are on display at The Chapin Library of Rare Books and Manuscripts.

John Dickinson was the main author of both the Articles of Confederation and the Olive Branch Petition.

Congress until 1777. John Dickinson was the main author of the articles.

Congress created the Articles of Confederation to unite the states for certain purposes. Most important among these was fighting the Revolutionary War against Great Britain. The states would have to work together to win the war.

Weaknesses of the Articles of Confederation

The Articles of Confederation had several problems. Congress could not create or collect taxes. This meant the government had little power to raise money. It also did not have the power to control trade between states and with other countries. Congress could make laws but it had no power to enforce them.

State Governments

The Articles of Confederation held the states together during the Revolutionary War. But the state governments continued to hold most of the power.

Virginia created a constitution in 1776. This became a model for the other states. It began with a declaration of rights. Many of the ideas from that document would become a part of the Bill of Rights the United States has today. Pennsylvania's constitution established yearly elections. Almost every man had the

Benjamin Franklin

Franklin played an important role in the creation of the United States. He helped write the Declaration of Independence. And he was an important member of the group that negotiated the Treaty of Paris. Franklin was also the oldest member of the Constitutional Convention. This group would write the Constitution of the United States.

Benjamin Franklin's work was essential to victory in the Revolutionary War and the formation of the United States of America.

right to vote. Massachusetts's constitution created strict separations between the different branches of government. They wanted to make sure no one part of the government became too powerful. These ideas would serve as important stepping stones for the structure the US government has today.

Victory for a New Nation

With help from France, the former colonists defeated Great Britain in 1781 in their war for independence. Great Britain recognized this independence in the

Treaty of Paris in 1783. The promise of the Declaration of Independence was now real.

The Articles of Confederation were too weak to govern the quickly changing United States. The writers of the Constitution would struggle to create an effective government that protected the rights of the states and the people.

FURTHER EVIDENCE

The Articles of Confederation held the former colonies together during the Revolutionary War. But the state governments were still independent. Review Chapter Two. Identify its main point and find supporting evidence. Then visit the Web site below to learn more about the balance between states' rights and the central government. Does it tell the story of this time in the same way as this book does? What differences can you find?

Articles of Confederation Submitted to the States

www.history.com/this-day-in-history/articles-of-confederation-submitted-to-the-states

CHAPTER THREE

The Constitutional Convention

The Constitutional Convention began in May 1787. Delegates from every state except Rhode Island attended. The purpose of this meeting was to rewrite the Articles of Confederation. Many of the delegates believed this was necessary to create a stronger central government.

The delegates met in Philadelphia under difficult conditions. The heat was awful. The insects were

George Washington presiding over the Constitutional Convention in 1787.

terrible. Most of these men had traveled long distances to reach the convention. They stayed in small rooms above taverns. Day after day, they discussed the issues related to creating a national government. It would take them nearly four months to write the Constitution. This document would define the rules that organize our nation.

Important Delegates

The 55 men who created the Constitution were among the most educated, powerful, and wealthy people of their time. They named George Washington as president of the convention. Washington was the former general of the colonial army. He would also become the first president of the United States. He spoke little during the debates. But his influence helped bring the delegates to a compromise.

James Madison provided ideas that served as the starting point for much of the Constitution. Madison went on to serve as a representative in the first US

James Madison was one of the main authors of the Constitution.

Congress. He would also become the fourth president of the United States.

After Madison, James Wilson was perhaps the most influential man at the convention. Wilson shared his great knowledge of other governments throughout history. This helped to shape the thoughts of the delegates as they wrote the Constitution.

George Mason was a southerner. Yet he fought against slavery at the convention. He also disagreed with creating a strong central government. His ideas influenced the later addition of a Bill of Rights to the Constitution.

The title page of
*The Federalist
Papers*, written by
Alexander
Hamilton, James
Madison, and
John Jay.

THE

FEDERALIST:

ADDRESSED TO THE

PEOPLE OF THE STATE OF
NEW-YORK.

Federalists vs. Anti-Federalists

The delegates fell into two main groups. Federalists believed a strong central government would be necessary for their growing nation. They wanted to create a system of checks and balances. This would prevent any one part of the government from becoming too powerful. For example, the president would be commander in chief of the military. But Congress had the power to declare war.

Anti-Federalists feared a strong central government. They thought it would threaten the rights of both the states and individuals. Anti-Federalists did not want a new constitution.

They wanted to change the Articles of Confederation instead.

They had many worries. Some worried the position of president might lead to one man becoming as powerful as a king. Others wanted the states to be more powerful than the national government.

Writing the Constitution took several months of discussion and argument between these two groups. Delegates considered many plans for the new government before reaching a compromise.

The Virginia Plan

Madison drew up a set of ideas named the Virginia Plan. It called for a new constitution. He wanted

The Publius Essays

Hamilton, Madison, and John Jay were important Federalists. They wrote a series of essays known as *The Federalist Papers* in support of the new constitution. The 85 essays explained the meaning and strengths of the proposed government. The men published these essays in newspapers under the pen name, "Publius."

a strong central government made up of three branches. The legislative branch would have two houses. This branch would elect an executive officer for a single term.

The New Jersey Plan

William Paterson introduced the New Jersey Plan. It called for a set of resolutions that would change and strengthen the Articles of Confederation. This plan would give greater powers to the Congress. It would also divide the government into three branches. But it called for two executives instead of one.

The Great Compromise

The delegates considered these plans and several others. They came to a compromise that combined the New Jersey and Virginia Plans. They agreed to a law-making body with two parts.

The compromise based the number of members sent by each state to the House of Representatives on population. This idea came from the Virginia Plan.

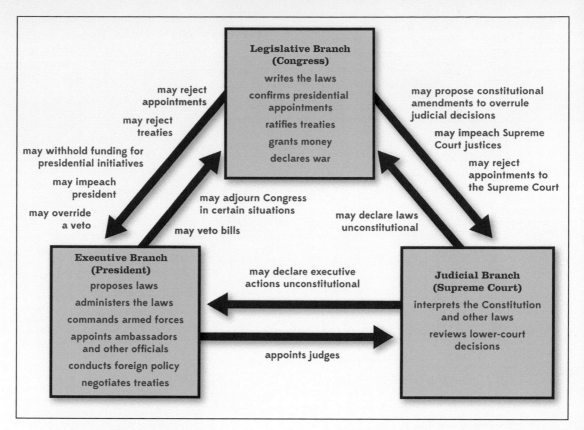

Legislative Branch (Congress)
- writes the laws
- confirms presidential appointments
- ratifies treaties
- grants money
- declares war

may reject appointments

may reject treaties

may withhold funding for presidential initiatives

may impeach president

may override a veto

may adjourn Congress in certain situations

may veto bills

may propose constitutional amendments to overrule judicial decisions

may impeach Supreme Court justices

may reject appointments to the Supreme Court

may declare laws unconstitutional

may declare executive actions unconstitutional

Executive Branch (President)
- proposes laws
- administers the laws
- commands armed forces
- appoints ambassadors and other officials
- conducts foreign policy
- negotiates treaties

appoints judges

Judicial Branch (Supreme Court)
- interprets the Constitution and other laws
- reviews lower-court decisions

Checks and Balances

The Constitution divided our government into three branches. Each branch would have power over certain aspects of the other two. This chart shows some of the checks and balances built into the US government. Does any branch seem stronger than another? Why or why not? Use facts from the chart to support your argument.

There would be one representative for every 30,000 people in a state. The compromise also said that each state would have two senators. This suggestion came from the New Jersey Plan.

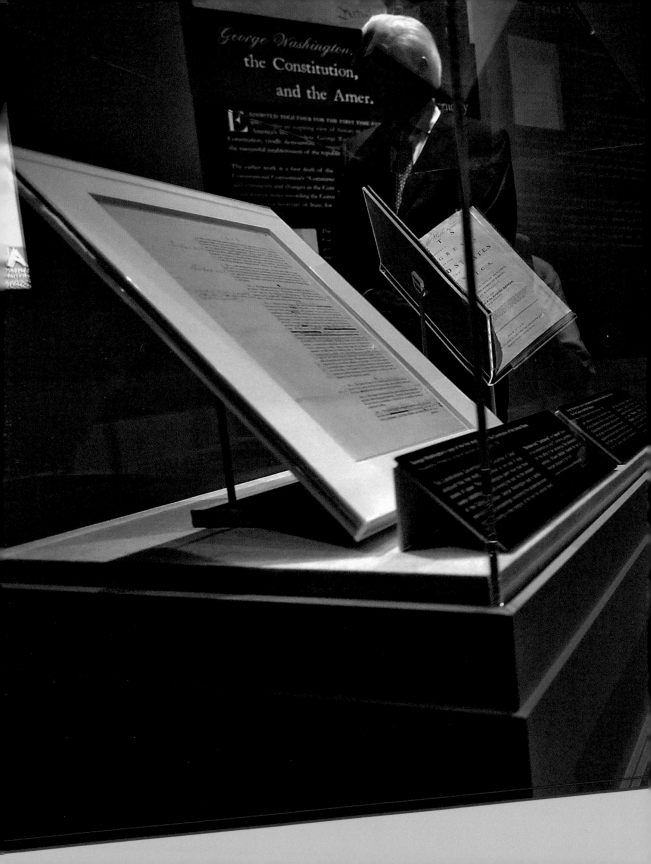

CHAPTER FOUR

Writing the Constitution

The delegates had reached the Great Compromise. But they still had many things to explain in the Constitution. What could the legislature do? What role would the court system play? How would the new nation choose its president? And how would they deal with the issue of slavery?

George Washington's personal copy of the US Constitution and Bill of Rights is on display at the Mount Vernon Estate.

The 110th Congress is sworn in on January 4, 2007. The rules created by the Constitution still govern how we elect our Congress members today.

The Legislative Branch

The delegates split the government into three branches. The legislative branch includes the House of Representatives and the Senate. This branch makes laws. It also creates and collects taxes, maintains the military, manages foreign affairs and trade, declares war, and maintains a post office.

The Constitution notes that voters in each state elect representatives every two years. A representative has to be at least 25 years old and has to have been a US citizen for at least seven years. Senators have to be at least 30 years old and a citizen for at least nine years. Both senators and representatives must live in the states that elect them.

The Executive Branch

The executive branch includes the president and the vice president. Although it is not mentioned in the Constitution, the executive branch also includes the president's cabinet members and other government agencies.

The Constitution notes the president serves a four-year term. Having a leader with such a limited time in office was very different from most other governments during that period. The authors of the Constitution were cautious about putting too much power into any one person's hands.

The Constitution also says the president serves as commander in chief of the military. The president must give Congress information about the "State of the Union" from time to time.

The justices of the US Supreme Court in 2010. The Supreme Court rules on whether laws are in agreement with the rules set forth in the Constitution.

To be elected president, candidates must have been born in the United States. They must also have parents who were both citizens. They must be at least 35 years old and have lived in the United States for at least 14 years.

The Judicial Branch

The authors of the Constitution created the Supreme Court. It first met in 1790. The authors gave Congress the power to create lower courts. The Supreme Court deals with cases affected by the Constitution. The Constitution says the president nominates Supreme

Court judges. Congress then approves these judges. Once approved, Supreme Court justices usually serve for life.

The Constitution says all citizens will receive a jury trial if accused of a crime. It also says all trials will take place in the state where the crime is said to have happened.

The Three-Fifths Rule

Many of the men who created the Constitution were against slavery. But the southern states depended on the unpaid work

Slavery and the Constitution

In the Declaration of Independence, Jefferson wrote, "all men are created equal." Yet many of the men who wrote the Constitution owned slaves. Some believed slavery went against the ideal of liberty on which our nation was founded. But slavery was important to the southern states. Some delegates argued against ending slavery. They wanted the southern states to approve the Constitution. The delegates' commitment to creating a unified nation won out over protests against slavery. But several delegates, including Franklin and Hamilton, worked to end slavery in their own states.

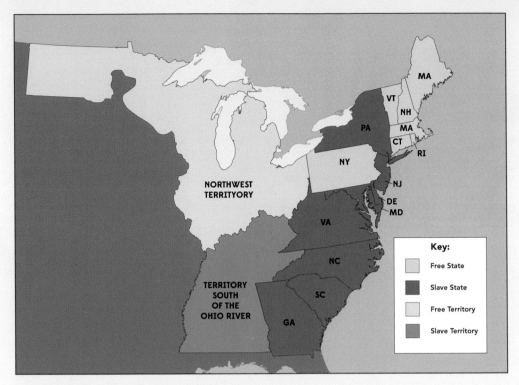

The Geography of Slavery

This map shows the areas of the United States that did and did not have slavery in 1787 when the Constitution was written. What does it tell you about the power of the slave states at the Constitutional Convention? Why did the delegates need to make sure the southern states would approve the Constitution?

of slaves. How would slaves be counted when determining how many people lived in a state? This number was important because it determined how many members each state would send to the House of Representatives.

Most of the southern delegates wanted to count each slave as one person. This would give their states more votes in the House of Representatives. Others argued that only free people should be counted. The delegates agreed to a compromise suggested by James Wilson and Roger Sherman. They decided to count each slave as three-fifths of a free person.

The Detail Committee

When the delegates felt they had finished the Constitution, a detail committee created a draft of the document. They gave names to the branches of the government. They also added the Preamble. This important part of the Constitution says the government exists to serve the people.

The Final Draft

After the detail committee finished, the delegates met for another five weeks of debate. They had settled many issues with the Great Compromise. But they still had to make decisions on several matters.

It would take months of debate and argument for the delegates at the Constitutional Convention to complete the Constitution.

One change the delegates discussed was the addition of a bill of rights. This would guarantee Americans certain personal freedoms. Some delegates believed it was important to define these rights. Others thought the Constitution already addressed these issues. After months of work, many of the delegates simply wanted to go home. They decided to drop the issue. Several Anti-Federalists were against this decision.

Thirty-nine of the 55 delegates signed the finished Constitution on September 17, 1787. Congress would now send it to the states for approval.

Benjamin Franklin's Speech to the Convention

Franklin wrote a short speech to be read before the delegates signed the Constitution. He hoped it would create a sense of unity among the men trying to create their new nation.

I confess that there are several parts of this constitution which I do not at present approve, but I am not sure I shall never approve them: For having lived long, I have experienced many instances of being obliged by better information. . . . to change opinions even on important subjects, which I once thought right, but found to be otherwise. . . . I can not help expressing a wish that every member of the Convention who may still have objections to it, would with me, on this occasion doubt a little of his own infallibility. . . . put his name to this instrument.

Source: Benjamin Franklin. "Speech of Benjamin Franklin." 1787. U.S. Constitution. Craig Walenta, 2010. Web. Accessed November 13, 2012.

Consider Your Audience

Read the passage above closely. How could you adapt its message for a modern audience, such as your neighbors or classmates? Write a blog post giving this same information to a new audience. What is the most effective way to get your point across to this audience? How is the language you use for the new audience different from the original text? Why?

CHAPTER FIVE

The Bill of Rights and Other Amendments

After months of argument and compromise, the delegates sent the Constitution to the states for approval. This was not an easy process. Some states would not approve the document without the addition of a bill of rights.

The first US Congress created the Bill of Rights in 1789. This document was a list of 12 amendments, or additions, to the Constitution. The states then

A parade on Wall Street in New York City honored Alexander Hamilton and the new US Constitution in 1787. The parade float pictured represented the "Ship of State."

The Massachusetts Ratifying Convention

Massachusetts's convention to approve the US Constitution was full of fierce debate. The president of the convention, John Hancock, was against a strong central government and wanted a bill of rights added. Samuel Adams had clashed with Hancock in the past. But the two came together to support these issues. The convention approved the Constitution by a close vote. But it also demanded the addition of several amendments. Other states followed Massachusetts's lead. These demands led in part to the creation of the Bill of Rights.

approved ten of those amendments in 1791. These became the Bill of Rights.

The Bill of Rights defines the rights held by the people of the United States. Its authors wanted Americans to know their government belongs to them. This was very different from the style of government the colonists had lived under as citizens of Great Britain.

The Bill of Rights lists things the government cannot do to take away the individual

John Hancock was an important force behind the addition of the Bill of Rights to the Constitution.

rights and freedoms of American citizens. The First Amendment guarantees freedom of speech, freedom of the press, and the freedom to choose one's own religion. It also guarantees the right of citizens to gather peacefully to protest. The Second Amendment guarantees the right to bear arms. The Third Amendment limits the government's ability to make citizens provide food and housing for soldiers.

This was something the British government had done before the Revolutionary War. The Fourth Amendment forbids illegal searches of citizens' homes. It also forbids the removal of papers or other items from private property without a warrant. The Fifth, Sixth, Seventh, and Eighth Amendments all define the rights of those accused of a crime.

The rights and freedoms guaranteed by the Bill of Rights are an important part of our nation's ideals. You have the freedom to say whatever you like about the president. You can gather in public and protest with others who share your opinions. The First Amendment protects those freedoms.

Later Amendments

Changing the Constitution is difficult. To add an Amendment to the Constitution, both the House and Senate must approve it with a two-thirds vote. Then 38 of the 50 states must also approve it. More than 12,000 amendments have been suggested since the creation of the Bill of Rights. Congress has only sent

Protesters exercise their right to demonstrate against the government.

33 to the states for approval. Twenty-seven have passed.

Amendments have made important changes to the Constitution. These often reflect changes in our society and its ideas about equality. For instance, the Thirteenth Amendment ended slavery in 1865. Other amendments gave women and African-American men the right to vote.

The US Constitution is on display in the rotunda of the Library of Congress.

The Constitution Today

American life and society were very different when the Constitution was created. Lawmakers and politicians sometimes have trouble applying its ideas to present-day issues. Americans often disagree about what the writers of this document intended. But it is still the foundation of our government. This document is more than two centuries old. But it still controls much of how our government works today.

The Fifth Amendment

Congress added the Bill of Rights to the Constitution to protect citizens' personal freedoms and limit the government's power. The First Amendment lays out some of our most important freedoms as American citizens.

> *Congress shall make no law respecting an establishment of religion, or prohibiting the free exercise thereof . . . or abridging the freedom of speech, or of the press . . . or the right of the people peaceably to assemble, and to petition the Government for a redress of grievances.*
>
> Source: "The First Amendment." About.com. About.com: Civil Liberties, n.d. Web. Accessed November 13, 2012.

Changing Minds

This passage defines a set of personal freedoms and limits on government power. Take a position on how much freedom you believe citizens should have. Then, imagine your best friend has the opposite opinion. Write a short essay trying to change your friend's mind. Make sure you state your opinion and your reasons for it. Include facts and details that support your opinion.

IMPORTANT DATES

1774

The First Continental Congress meets in Philadelphia.

1775

The Revolutionary War begins on April 19.

1775

The Second Continental Congress meets beginning in May.

1783

The Treaty of Paris is signed, ending the Revolutionary War and acknowledging American independence from Great Britain.

1787

The Constitutional Convention drafts the Constitution between May 25 and September 17.

1789

The first US Congress meets and writes the Bill of Rights.

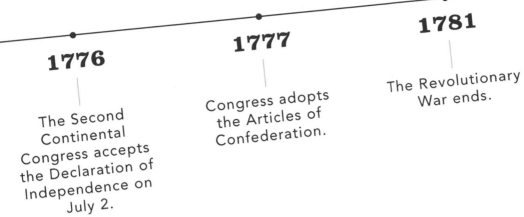

1776

The Second Continental Congress accepts the Declaration of Independence on July 2.

1777

Congress adopts the Articles of Confederation.

1781

The Revolutionary War ends.

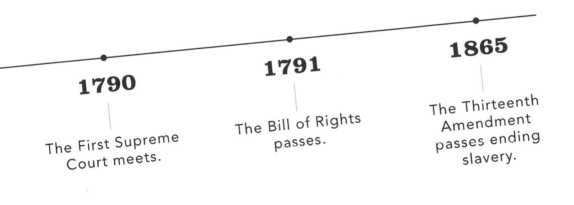

1790

The First Supreme Court meets.

1791

The Bill of Rights passes.

1865

The Thirteenth Amendment passes ending slavery.

You Are There

Imagine you are one of the delegates trying to come to the Great Compromise discussed in the book. Write a letter to a family member telling him or her about your experience. Which of the issues being debated is the most important to you, and why? What is it like living in Philadelphia while you are participating in this important event?

Tell the Tale

This book discusses how the delegates at the Constitutional Convention set about creating a document that still governs the United States today. Write 200 words that tell the true tale of how these men brought together their ideas about the best way to organize a new government. Be sure to set the scene, develop a sequence of events, and offer a conclusion.

Say What?

Find five words in this book you have never seen or heard before. Find out what they mean. Then write the meaning in your own words. Use each word in a sentence.

Take a Stand

This book discusses the Bill of Rights. Take a position on the Second Amendment and write a short essay explaining your opinion. State the reasons behind it. Be sure to include facts to support your position.

GLOSSARY

colony
a community settled in a new area that is governed by a parent country

constitution
a document establishing the form and powers of a government

delegate
a person who represents a group, especially in a government setting

draft
a rough version of a piece of writing from which a final version may be produced

Parliament
the law-making body of Great Britain

patriot
a person who loves his or her country and acts for its interests

preamble
a special introduction to a larger statement or piece of writing

revolution
to overthrow or consider a ruler or government no longer in charge of an area or country

tax
money paid to a governing body

treaty
an agreement between two or more parties about peace, trade, or other relations

LEARN MORE

Books

Espinosa, Rod. *George Washington*. Edina, MN: ABDO Publishing, 2008. Print.

Green, Meg, and Paula M. Stathakis. *The Everything Founding Father Book*. Avon, MA: Adams Media, 2011. Print.

Murray, Stuart. *Eyewitness: American Revolution*. London: DK Publishing, 2005. Print.

Web Links

To learn more about the Constitution and the Bill of Rights, visit ABDO Publishing Company online at **www.abdopublishing.com**. Web sites about the Constitution are featured on our Book Links page. These links are routinely monitored and updated to provide the most current information available. Visit **www.mycorelibrary.com** for free additional tools for teachers and students.

INDEX

ABOUT THE AUTHOR

Maegan Schmidt is a freelance writer with an M.A. in literature from the University of St. Thomas, and a B.A. in literature from Chatham College. Maegan lives in Hastings, Minnesota, with her husband and three kids.